You Are There!

Pearl Harbor
December 7, 1941

Dona Herweck Rice

Consultants

Timothy Rasinski, Ph.D.
Kent State University

Lori Oczkus, M.A.
Literacy Consultant

Publishing Credits

Rachelle Cracchiolo, M.S.Ed., *Publisher*
Conni Medina, M.A.Ed., *Managing Editor*
Dona Herweck Rice, *Series Developer*
Emily R. Smith, M.A.Ed., *Content Director*
Seth Rogers/Noelle Cristea, M.A.Ed., *Editors*
Robin Erickson, *Senior Graphic Designer*

The TIME logo is a registered trademark of TIME Inc. Used under license.

Image Credits: Cover and p.1 GL Archive/Alamy Stock Photo;
pp.2–3 Lebrecht Music and Arts Photo Library/Alamy Stock Photo;
pp.4–5 Epics/Getty Images; pp.10–11 Popperfoto/Getty Images;
pp.12–13 SPUTNIK/Alamy Stock Photo; p.13 LOC [LC-USZ62-108206];
pp.14–15 Google Earth; p.16 (bottom) World History Archive/Alamy
Stock Photo; pp.16–17 Bob Cornelis/Getty Images; pp. 18–19 NARA
[295976]; pp.20–21, 22–23, 24–25 Granger, NYC; pp.26–27 Douglas
Peebles Photography/Alamy Stock Photo; all other images from
iStock and/or Shutterstock

Teacher Created Materials

5301 Oceanus Drive
Huntington Beach, CA 92649-1030
http://www.tcmpub.com

ISBN 978-1-4938-3928-5

© 2017 Teacher Created Materials, Inc.
Printed in China
Nordica.072018.CA21800845

Table of Contents

December Day in Hawai'i

The sun rises over the calm and quiet United States Naval Base at Pearl Harbor on the island of O'ahu, Hawai'i. It is Sunday, and many of the military men and women are on leave for the weekend. Most offices and shops are closed. Still, the base hums as the **military personnel** stationed there go about their daily routines, whether servicing the vessels and planes that are critical to U.S. military strength or simply enjoying some much-deserved leisure.

The U.S. military is growing in strength, developing the means and training to protect and defend the nation it serves. Knowing that wars are being **waged** brutally in Europe and the Pacific, U.S. armed forces are prepared, despite the nation's desire to stay isolated from the wars that seemingly have little to do with its concerns. The military is ready to deploy if it needs to. But government leaders are clear: this is not America's war.

The base wakes up that day under an expanse of blue sky, dotted with clouds. The sun shines brightly, and temperatures are expected to reach into the 80s. The military personnel have hopes of enjoying some of the Hawai'ian sunshine before day's end. Plenty of folks back home on the mainland might be deep in snow and cold about this time, but December in Hawai'i is almost always a paradise.

Typical Day

Former Navy Captain Douglas G. Phillips, who was stationed at Pearl Harbor during the attack, later recounted, "I remember very well what I was doing [that morning]. It was my first day aboard. It was a beautiful sunny day. I was up and had breakfast—first one in the **wardroom**. Then I was up on deck admiring the scenery and was pretty happy."

aerial view of Pearl Harbor

At Service

On December 7, 1941, 17,567 men and 234 women were stationed at Pearl Harbor. Of the women, 200 were nurses.

Out of the Blue

On this day, the necessary staff of sailors, soldiers, mechanics, nurses, and service people are at work bright and early, doing their duty for the country they serve. Although operating in smaller numbers than on a typical weekday, there is still a rhythm to their work, as befits any military station. Everyone can be counted on to do what he or she is tasked to do exactly when tasked to do it. In the military, you can rely on people and systems operating as expected. It's fundamental and essential. The men and women at Pearl Harbor certainly know this to be true.

Except on this day—December 7, 1941—it isn't. An unexpected sound breaks through the familiar clangs and hums of the station. It is the sound of engines in the air, coming in fast and low. The engines grow louder and louder until, dropping from the blue, a swarm of Japanese fighter planes thunders across the sky—and, without warning to the people of O'ahu, rain destruction on Pearl Harbor.

Spy

Takeo Yoshikawa was a Japanese spy who reported from Hawai'i while posing as a **diplomat**. Through telegraph codes, he advised that the morning of December 7 would be an ideal time to attack, since many ships and planes would be docked and grounded at the harbor. In destroying them, Japan hoped to cripple the U.S. military.

Detected but Mistaken

A radar system with cutting-edge technology was newly in place at Opana Point on the north shore of O'ahu. The radar did what it was supposed to do—detect the incoming planes. However, they were mistaken for American planes. An army lieutenant who was notified of the sighting told the **privates** on duty, "Well, don't worry about it."

Before the Attack

Let's push pause here.

To understand what happened on that **infamous** December day on the island paradise of Hawai'i, it's important to look at everything leading to it. Why Hawai'i? Why Pearl Harbor? And why did the Japanese attack?

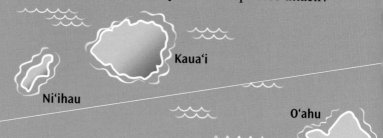

People have called the Hawai'ian islands home for centuries. Before Europeans discovered Hawai'i, the people there lived under a monarchy and shared a rich culture. Traditional stories offer many explanations for how the islands were formed and how life evolved. One story is of the goddess Ka'ahupāhau who is said to protect Pearl Harbor. She was born human but transformed into a shark. She and her son (or brother—stories vary), Kahi'ukā, live in a cave at the harbor and protect the people and sea life from dangerous invaders.

'Okina

In the Hawai'ian language, there is a letter that looks similar to an apostrophe. It's called an 'okina. The 'okina indicates a glottal stop, or brief pause. Think of the word "uh-oh." The break in the syllables is a glottal stop.

The harbor was known as Wai Momi, "Water of Pearl," and was sometimes called Pu'uloa, "Long Hill." Until the twentieth century, when industrialization took root, it was rich with oysters and pearls.

In 1778, Captain James Cook of Britain sailed past the harbor, leaving it undisturbed. But in 1793, Captain William Brown sailed into the harbor on the *Butterworth*. He named the port Fair Haven.

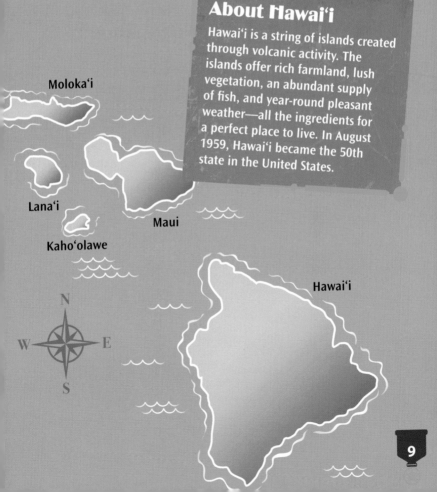

About Hawai'i

Hawai'i is a string of islands created through volcanic activity. The islands offer rich farmland, lush vegetation, an abundant supply of fish, and year-round pleasant weather—all the ingredients for a perfect place to live. In August 1959, Hawai'i became the 50th state in the United States.

Moloka'i

Lana'i

Maui

Kaho'olawe

Hawai'i

N
W E
S

Western Control

Through the next century, Europe and the United States explored Hawai'i to capitalize on its resources. Over time, they also saw the value of its location from a military point of view.

In 1887, the Kingdom of Hawai'i renewed a treaty with the United States. In it, the United States gained control of Pearl Harbor, while Hawai'ians could sell their sugar **duty-free** on the U.S. mainland. When the Hawai'ian monarchy was overthrown in 1893, the United States gained even more than this limited control. In 1898, Hawai'i was **annexed** as a U.S. **territory**. The United States now had a vital military hold in the Pacific.

Schofield Barracks

In 1908, Schofield Barracks was built at Pearl Harbor. At the time, it was the largest U.S. Army post.

Once Hawai'i was annexed, the United States began to improve the harbor, providing easy access for large ships. That meant **dredging** the harbor and destroying the coral, which angered many of the local people. The work was **beset** with challenges. Locals said it was Ka'ahupāhau and Kahi'ukā at work, angry over the threat to their home.

In 1917, Ford Island—at the heart of Pearl Harbor—became a military base for the U.S. Navy. As Japan's military strength grew, the United States depended more and more on Pearl Harbor. Much of the U.S. fleet was docked there, ready to sail into action. In 1935, Hickam Field was built near Ford Island as a state-of-the-art army air station. The U.S. presence and power in Pearl Harbor was secure.

Coral

Many people think coral is a plant or even a type of rock. Neither is true. Coral is formed by a compact colony of **invertebrates** and is an important part of its ecosystem.

From California to Hawai'i

In 1940, with the growing threat of Japanese **imperialism**, President Franklin D. Roosevelt decided to step up U.S. military presence in Pearl Harbor. California had been a naval stronghold for the Pacific, but Pearl Harbor was in a much more **strategic** location. Nearly the entire Pacific Fleet was moved from California to its new home in Pearl Harbor.

The Empire of Japan saw this move as a threat. The U.S. military was nearer than it had ever been to Japan. The Empire sought to expand its global presence and power. The United States was now close enough to **meddle** with Japan's quest to expand into mainland Asia.

As World War II waged elsewhere, few U.S. leaders thought an attack on Pearl Harbor was likely. An attack on American soil seemed foolhardy, given U.S. military strength as well as the enormous distance between Japan and the United States. Pearl Harbor and all its holdings seemed quite secure. Until they weren't.

China Factor

Growing tensions between Japan and the United States were due in part to Japan's invasion of China in 1937. The United States tried to lessen Japanese aggression by withholding money and goods—especially oil. Diplomatic negotiations between the nations went nowhere. War seemed unavoidable.

Think Link

- Why would a military stronghold in the Pacific be important for the United States?
- How might the United States have been seen as a threat to the Empire of Japan?
- For what reasons was the United States trying to stay out of WWII?

Franklin D. Roosevelt

Mapping Pearl Harbor

To fully understand the attack and the strategic position of Pearl Harbor, take a look at the harbor itself as well as its location in the world.

Pearl Harbor

An Eye on Pearl Harbor

By December 7, 1941, almost every ship in the Pacific Fleet was based at Pearl Harbor. Hundreds of airplanes were stationed at its airfields. To succeed in the destruction of Pearl Harbor would be a huge military advantage for any invader.

Data USGS

CANADA

JAPAN

UNITED
STATES

MEXICO

NORTH
PACIFIC
OCEAN

NORTH
PACIFIC
OCEAN

U.S.
Hawaiian
islands

Bering Sea

Sea
of
Okhotsk

Philippine
Sea

Honolulu

Waikiki

Google ea

"A Date Which Will Live in Infamy"

Now, let's press play.

It is just past 7:00 a.m., December 7, and about 50 Japanese aircraft are in flight to the island of O'ahu. The Opana Point radar picks up their signals, but the planes are misidentified as U.S. bombers. The Japanese bombers fly on, unchallenged.

Across the country in Washington, DC, government leaders receive news from military code breakers. They've just decoded a message to all Japanese negotiators working with the United States. The Japanese are directed to stop all negotiations regarding China and leave immediately.

In Washington, military leaders are on high alert. They are confident this move means war is **imminent**. They race to warn the U.S. armed forces commander in Hawai'i, Lieutenant General Walter Short. But static in the air prevents all messages from getting through to the islands. The warning is sent by telegraph but will not reach Short's office until about 11:45 a.m., and he won't see it until well into the afternoon. There might as well have been no warning at all.

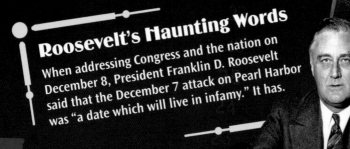

Roosevelt's Haunting Words

When addressing Congress and the nation on December 8, President Franklin D. Roosevelt said that the December 7 attack on Pearl Harbor was "a date which will live in infamy." It has.

Cryptography

Cryptography—the making and breaking of codes for purposes of communication—was used throughout World War II to send messages to allies and keep important information from falling into the wrong hands.

Submarine Spotted

The U.S. destroyer ship *Ward* sighted a Japanese submarine attempting to cross into the harbor. The ship fired on the sub and reported what happened to Admiral Husband Kimmel, the commander of the Pacific Fleet. Kimmel had dealt with many similar reports that turned out to be false, so he decided to take no action until this report could be validated.

Aircraft Carriers Come into Play

At 7:40 a.m., the swarm of bombers, torpedo planes, and fighter planes approach the island in the Pacific. The 183 aircraft hide above a layer of clouds to approach Oʻahu unseen. After all, in an attack of war, the element of surprise is everything.

Mitsuo Fuchida is the Japanese commander of the air attack, and he worries that the cloud cover will obscure the harbor and prevent their mission. But as the clouds break, Fuchida can see there are no U.S. aircraft carriers visible on the water. The Japanese won't be able to destroy the Pacific Fleet's carriers as hoped, but the empty waters confirm that no one anticipates their approach.

At 7:49 a.m., Fuchida gives the order: *"To, to, to!"* This was the signal for pilots to attack. Fuchida follows this message with a second coded message, *"To ra, to ra, to ra,"* meaning "attack; surprise achieved." With those simple words, the massive, unexpected, and **harrowing** air strike begins.

When Commander Logan Ramsey, stationed on Ford Island, sees the first bomb fall at 7:55 a.m., he directs station operators to send a wide-reaching telegraph. Because it is urgent and there is no time for translation, he does not encode the message. It reads simply, "AIR RAID ON PEARL HARBOR X THIS IS NOT DRILL."

Tora

On this mission, *to ra* meant "attack; surprise achieved." In Japanese, the word *tora* means "tiger." This coincidence has caused a lot of confusion over the decades. The origins of these code words continue to be a subject of debate.

Secret Weapon

Japan developed special finned torpedoes for the attack. They were designed to be dropped from planes and level out a few feet under the water. Regular torpedoes would have gotten stuck in the sea floor due to the shallow water in the harbor.

Strike!

The sky explodes! Bombs fall in a devastating firestorm. First targeted are the rows of planes at Wheeler Field and Hickam Field. The aircraft are obvious **marks,** having been stored in neat rows. It's almost too easy. The Japanese bombers intend to dominate the skies during wartime by destroying as many U.S. military planes as possible, and they are well on their way to success. The planes at Wheeler and Hickam are nearly **annihilated**.

At 8:00 a.m., the expected U.S. planes arrive—the ones that the Japanese planes had been mistaken for—but their pilots are ignorant of the attack. While attempting to land at Oʻahu, they instead must evade Japanese bombs as well as return gunfire. Miraculously, they escape almost untouched.

Just minutes later, the worst devastation comes not only in the destruction of aircraft and ships, but also in loss of life—loss in staggering numbers. A bomb designed to pierce armor is dropped from above and easily rips through the battleship *Arizona*. A massive amount of gunpowder ignites, shooting an explosive fireball through the ship and into the air. The United States ship (USS) *Arizona* is sunk within minutes, killing 1,177 sailors and marines. Many were trapped by both fire and sea.

Act of Bravery

Dorie Miller became the first African American to be awarded the Navy Cross, the U.S. Navy's highest service award. At profound risk to his own safety, he assisted his gravely injured captain and then operated a machine gun, which he was not well trained to do.

A Sailor's Story

U.S. Naval Reserve officer George Macartney Hunter, present during the attack, recorded in his journal, "We had been under attack for 15 minutes at this time and the harbor was a living hell. **Astern** of us the *Arizona*'s forward magazine had blown up . . . Smoke was spreading rapidly over the harbor. Very shortly the day became black as night; it was terrifying beyond means of description."

As bombs fall and torpedoes blast, U.S. forces scramble to counterattack. The USS *Monaghan* blasts a Japanese submarine, rams it at full speed, and drops **charges**. A second wave of bombers strikes at 8:54 a.m. About 30 minutes later, a blast to the destroyer *Shaw* sends chunks of the ship a distance of half a mile (800 meters). The USS *Shaw* is crippled, but it will be repaired and back in service less than a year later.

U.S. forces are able to strike down about 15 Japanese planes, and through other means, the Japanese lose a total of 29. But the devastation to the men and women of Pearl Harbor is severe. In all, more than 2,403 people die and more than 1,178 are wounded. There is not enough medical staff or equipment to treat everyone. Some dying men are given **morphine** to dull their pain. Nurses mark Ms on their foreheads with lipstick to show they've been medicated. The morphine is often the only comfort they receive before dying.

In addition to the USS *Arizona*, the USS *Utah* and the USS *Oklahoma* were also destroyed. But every other struck vessel—even those that sunk—will eventually be lifted out of the water and repaired to sail again. In fact, many are instrumental in the eventual American defeat of the Japanese after many years of devastating war.

Buried with Comrades

There were more than 300 survivors of the sinking of the USS *Arizona*. In honor of their survival, these men can choose to be buried with their fallen shipmates. A special ceremony is held, and their ashes are placed into the ship.

Another Sailor's Story

In a 2013 interview, Navy veteran Richard Pena said this of his experience at Pearl Harbor: "You go into an automatic mode. You go into what you've been taught to do, what you've been trained to do . . . but, at the same time, you're realizing that life is no longer the same." Pena explained, too, that it wasn't until Christmas that he was able to get word to his mother that he was alive.

"Awaken a Sleeping Giant"

At 1:00 p.m., the Japanese strike force leaves Pearl Harbor. The wounded are treated, and the dead are honored. Government leaders are **apprised** of the attack and begin to make plans. No longer is the United States a bystander to the wars raging throughout the world.

On December 8, 1941, President Roosevelt addresses Congress. Around the country, people listen on their radios. He tells the nation that the United States is now at war with the Empire of Japan. On December 11, Germany and Italy, Japan's allies, declare war on the United States. The United States declares war in return.

Satisfaction

When the Japanese surrendered in 1945, the USS *West Virginia*, one of the ships that was attacked, was present.

The U.S. response is quick, and troops are immediately deployed. The people of the United States are passionate in their **resolve** to avenge Pearl Harbor and obliterate what they consider to be evil in the world. Young men and women **enlist** or are **drafted** into military service. People everywhere join together to support the war effort. In the blink of an eye, the United States is fully and completely at war.

Seeing the swift and powerful U.S. response, Japanese Admiral Isoroku Yamamoto is said to declare, "I fear all we have done is to awaken a sleeping giant and fill him with terrible resolve."

	United States	Japan
Fatalities	2,335 military; 68 civilian	64
Wounded	1,143 military; 35 civilian	unknown
Ships Destroyed	3	5
Ships Damaged	16	unknown
Aircraft Destroyed	169	29
Aircraft Damaged	159	74

STOP! THINK...

This chart shows the approximate numbers of casualties and property loss at Pearl Harbor. Read it and consider the questions.

◎ How does the loss of life on the USS *Arizona* (1,177 crew killed) compare to the fatalities in the entire attack?

◎ Why was the attack on Pearl Harbor so motivating for the U.S. government and people as far as entering the war was concerned?

◎ Why are some of the numbers for Japan unknown?

In the aftermath of Pearl Harbor, anti-Japanese sentiment runs high in the United States. All Japanese people are linked with the attackers in the public's eye. But many thousands of people of Japanese descent live in the United States. The majority are American citizens. Fear and fury run so high, though, that more than 120,000 Japanese Americans are stripped of their belongings, including their homes and businesses. They are forced to move to "relocation centers" by Executive Order of the president. The centers are overcrowded and dirty, and people are given limited **rations** of food to eat. Adults are offered the opportunity to be released if they enlist in the military. Some do. Detentions remain in effect until 1946.

The United States' involvement in the war lasts until its end. After **atom bombs** create unmatched devastation and loss of life in the Japanese cities of Hiroshima and Nagasaki in August 1945, the war comes to an end. On September 2, 1945, the Japanese signed the surrender papers. The streets of the United States—and the base at Pearl Harbor—erupt in celebration.

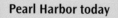

Pearl Harbor today

Pearl Harbor Today

It has been many years since the attack on Pearl Harbor. Millions of visitors pay tribute at the memorial each year, including countless Japanese tourists. In the end, the attack on Pearl Harbor proved devastating for all, Americans and Japanese alike. Peace between the nations has reigned since the last shots of the war were fired. Today, the nations are allies. But it is important that the lessons of Pearl Harbor and the war are never forgotten.

Battle of Ni'ihau

During the attack, a Japanese plane crashed on the island of Ni'ihau and the pilot was captured. But a Japanese person living there later assisted him by giving him weapons. On the run, the pilot and the local man kidnapped a couple that lived on the island. Luckily, the captors were overpowered and the couple escaped.

Glossary

annexed—took control of a territory by adding it as a dependent of a country

annihilated—wiped out

apprised—informed

astern—behind a ship

atom bombs—intense explosive devices with impacts far beyond traditional explosives, created by splitting atoms

beset—troubled

charges—bombs

diplomat—person who represents his or her country from within another country

drafted—called into military service

dredging—digging to deepen a waterway

duty-free—without taxation

enlist—sign up for military service

harrowing—very upsetting

imminent—happening very soon

imperialism—the practice by one country of forcibly gaining control of other, usually poorer, countries

infamous—well known for negative reasons

invertebrates—animals without spinal columns

marks—targets

meddle—to get involved without permission; interfere

military personnel—members of the armed forces

morphine—powerful painkilling medicine made from opium

privates—low-ranking members of the armed forces

rations—food allotted to a person or group

resolve—strong determination

stationed—placed by leaders for purposes of work and living

strategic—part of a plan designed to achieve a goal, especially a military or political one

territory—area of land that is controlled by a larger government

waged—carried on

wardroom—room on a military ship where officers eat and sleep

Index

Check It Out!

Books

Brennan Demuth, Patricia. 2013. *What Was Pearl Harbor?* Grosset & Dunlap.

Dougherty, Steve. 2009. *Pearl Harbor: The U.S. Enters World War II.* Scholastic.

Mazer, Harry. 2002. *A Boy at War: A Novel of Pearl Harbor.* Simon & Schuster Books for Young Readers.

———. 2006. *A Boy No More.* Simon & Schuster Books for Young Readers.

Van Der Vat, Dan. 2001. *Pearl Harbor: An Illustrated History.* Basic Books.

Videos

Bay, Michael. *Pearl Harbor.* Touchstone Pictures.

Fleischer, Richard, Kinji Fukasaku, and Toshio Masuda. *Tora! Tora! Tora!* 20th Century Fox.

Websites

A+E Networks Corporation. Pearl Harbor. http://www.history.com/topics/world-war-ii/pearl-harbor.

National Park Service. *World War II: Valor in the Pacific.* https://www.nps.gov/valr/index.htm.

Try It!

The attack on Pearl Harbor was one of the many events that took place during World War II. Imagine you are a cartoonist tasked with sketching a weeklong cartoon depicting a sequential record of other major events of World War II. To get started, you have some research to do:

- Research World War II. Make sure to look up the causes, allies, locations, important people, etc.

- List the major battles, events, and people involved on each side.

- Select seven major events and write them on a timeline.

- Focus on one event at a time and sketch a poster/scene detailing each event.

- Look back at your sketches to see if there are any additional details that you can add (scenery, labels, billboards, people, etc.).

- Write a caption (including the date) to attach to each image.

- Have a friend look over each sketch and suggest edits.

- Complete a final sketch (in color or digitally) of each event.

- Present your visual timeline to your class.

About the Author

Dona Herweck Rice has written hundreds of books, stories, and essays for kids on all kinds of topics, from pirates to heroes to why people have bad breath! Writing is her passion, but she also loves reading, live theater, dancing anytime and anywhere, and singing at the top of her lungs (although she'd be the first to tell you that this is not really a pleasure for anyone else). Rice was a teacher and is an acting coach. She lives in Southern California with her husband, two sons, and a cute but very silly little dog.